URBANOMICS 101

INTRODUCTION TO CREDIT AND BUSINESS

JZHAMAEL KEBULON ASHANTEE

URBANOMICS 101- INTRODUCTION TO CREDIT AND BUSINESS

COPYRIGHT © 2019 BY JZHAMAEL KEBULON ASHANTEE

ALL RIGHTS RESERVED. NO PART OF THIS PUBLICATION MAY BE REPRODUCED, DISTRIBUTED, OR TRANSMITTED IN ANY FORM OR BY ANY MEANS, INCLUDING PHOTOCOPYING, RECORDING, OR OTHER ELECTRONIC OR MECHANICAL METHODS, WITHOUT THE PRIOR WRITTEN PERMISSION OF THE PUBLISHER, EXCEPT IN THE CASE OF BRIEF QUOTATIONS EMBODIED IN CRITICAL REVIEWS AND CERTAIN OTHER NONCOMMERCIAL USES PERMITTED BY COPYRIGHT LAW. FOR PERMISSION REQUESTS, WRITE TO: JZHAMAEL K. ASHANTEE, ADDRESSED "ATTENTION: PERMISSIONS COORDINATOR," AT THE ADDRESS BELOW.

PUBLISHED BY:

URBANOMICS 101 INC. / JZHAMAEL K. ASHANTEE

P.O. BOX 716

PERRIS CALIFORNIA 92571 (USA)

WWW.URBANOMICS101.ORG

CONTACT: URBANOMICS101@YAHOO.COM

PUBLISHED IN UNITED STATES OF AMERICA.

DEDICATION

To my mom Priscilla Madlyn Lott and my grandmother Thelma Bunton Ford, thank you for your continuous love, support and encouragement.

ACKNOWLEDGEMENTS

I would like to thank all of the dedicated educators and advocates of financial freedom who have made it their life's mission to teach and promote self sufficiency through business, and through investing in the African American communities, our continent and throughout our entire diaspora.

This acknowledgement would not be complete without mentioning a few trailblazers of the past like Marcus Mosiah Garvey and Elijah Muhammad. I would also be remiss if I didn't give a special shout out to two of our biggest economics warriors today, Dr. Claud Anderson and Dr. Boyce Watkins.

My personal thanks to Aulsondro " Emcee Nice" Hamilton for our journey through music and animation.

James Thompkins founder and The Abakaus Group, for breaking the stock market code and sharing that knowledge with myself and others.

James Smith Moore, my personal eCommerce Guru.

CONTENTS

INTRODUCTION 6

PERSONAL CREDIT 8

BUSINESS/CORPORATE CREDIT 20

DEBT REDUCTION 33

INCORPORATING YOUR BUSINESS 52

ABOUT AUTHOR 58

INTRODUCTION

Welcome to the first book of the URBANOMICS 101 series on business and finance. These books have been researched and written to give you a friendly, easy-to-follow, step-by-step guide through the realms of starting your own business, getting a handle on your own finances, and investing your own money wisely. Way too many people go blindly forward without advice or a plan when it comes to establishing credit, creating a small business, or deciding how to invest money now for bigger payouts later. My goal in writing these books is to give you not only amazing insight into these subjects, but a clear, precise way of navigating different topics related to your money and your business that can serve as a template for you to achieve financial freedom, be the master of your own finances, and create a business that will allow you to live out your dreams.

In this first book, we'll start with the basics of getting yourself fiscally fit. Whether you are looking to start your own business, invest money for future purchases or your own retirement, or simply want to get to the point where you are financially sound, this is the book for you. As a bonus for all of you burgeoning entrepreneurs, we'll take a closer look at how you should create and structure your business organization to maximize your legal rights and minimizes your legal risks before you set up shop. The second book in this series focuses extensively on becoming your own boss and running your own company in the 21st century, so that final chapter is a great starting point to segue into thinking about yourself as a small business owner in the current digital environment.

01

PERSONAL CREDIT

Just like everything you do on the Internet, everything you do financially becomes part of who you are, for better or for worse. When you start having credit cards, loans, car notes, etc., you begin to register a credit score. This score can have both short- and long-term implications on how banks and other financial institutions view you.

WHAT IS IT?

Personal credit refers to your individual ability to buy and pay for things in a timely fashion. This is not about buying your weekly groceries or leaving a good tip at a restaurant, but how you operate when paying off your debts - such as personal/student loans, credit-card purchases, your car note, or your mortgage. Banks and other financial institutions carefully review this information when considering you for a loan.

WHAT DO I NEED IT FOR?

Before lending you money or giving you the ability to spend money beyond what you currently have, banks and credit-card companies want to be reasonably sure you have the ability and the history to pay them back on time. If you want to buy a house, and assuming you don't have enough cash to buy it outright, you'll need to apply for a home loan. In that instance, a bank buys the home and you begin making monthly payments to pay back the loan. The same process works when you want to buy a new car. If you're looking to start a business and don't have the capital to pay for everything upfront, you would apply for a business loan from a bank, which would then go through your financial records and your credit history to see how likely you are to repay the loan (plus interest) on time. Banks and other financial institutions use mathematical formulas to see if the level of risk involved with giving you a loan is acceptable or not.

HOW IS MY PERSONAL CREDIT SCORE CALCULATED?

A common misconception about your credit score is that it is based solely on whether or not you've missed payments on a previous loan. That can be a big factor in your score, but it is definitely not the only one. Thirty years ago, the FICO was introduced as the formula by which banks and other financial institutions measured an individual's creditworthiness. Equifax, Experian, and TransUnion are the three big consumer credit bureaus that collect your financial information to generate your score.

The formula for calculating that score has weighted percentages for different elements of credit and financial history including:

- **PAYMENT HISTORY: 35%**

This includes late payments, settlements, liens against you, repossessions, judgments, and filing for bankruptcy.

- **AMOUNTS OWED: 30%**

Several factors are at play here, including your debt-to-credit limit ratio. This is calculated by dividing your total credit-card debt by the total limit of your credit cards. For instance, if you have $15,000 of credit-card debt, but your total credit limit is $45,000, your debt ratio is at 33%. Other factors for this category include the actual amounts you owe, how many accounts have balances, and how much you are typically paying each month on each account.

- **LENGTH OF CREDIT HISTORY: 15%**

The older your accounts, the more likely it is that you're keeping them paid off, or at least down. The average age of your accounts will be factored here, as well as what the oldest account you have active.

- **TYPE OF CREDIT USED: 10%**

Banks want to see that you are using different types of credit for different types of purchases. They want to see the sort of stability that comes from purchasing a home or a car, not just several credit cards for department stores. Your ability to handle different types of credit makes you more likely to be financially responsible when it comes to your debts.

- **NEW CREDIT: 10%**

If you are struggling to pay off credit-card debt and keep switching balances to new cards with no interest, that will reflect poorly on your score. If you're making inquiries into rates for a mortgage or a student loan, this will not impact your score. It all depends on what your end-goal is.

WHAT DOES MY THREE-DIGIT CREDIT SCORE MEAN?

Once all the aforementioned factors have been taken into account, your FICO score is generated and shared with any financial organization that is considering lending you money. Scores range between 350-850 points and fall into different strata in terms of how likely you are to get a loan. But remember, the credit score is not the end-all, be-all of applying for a loan. Other factors such as having a large down payment for a house or car, or having a co-signer also can come into play. Here is a breakdown of the FICO scores:

- **579 OR LESS**

Bad: A credit score under 579 is considered too risky for most financial institutions unless it is a fairly short loan with high interest rates. A loan from the Small Business Administration (SBA) is generally thought to be out of the question at this level.

- **580-619**

Poor: A clear step-up from the previous category, and there are some financing options available, but those will have high interest rates attached.

- **620-679**

OK: This is the range that many Americans find themselves in. The SBA usually requires a score of at least 660 to contemplate a business loan, but the rates will not be the lowest. This is sort of a tipping point. If you manage your debt well, you can move up quickly from here, but if you spend unwisely you can expect the opposite to happen.

- **680-719**

Good: The average American settles in this range, which is great because it offers solid approvals and improved interest rates, making it easier to secure loans for homes, cars, and small businesses.

- **720-799**

Very good: Unless you're asking for $10 billion to build a full-scale model of the Death Star from "Star Wars", you're going to be good to go for just about any kind of loan with this score. Not only will excellent interest rates be made available, but additional perks as well, like better car insurance rates and not needing to pay security deposits on utilities.

- **800-850**

Excellent: You are truly in rarified air, and can expect banks and other lenders to treat you accordingly. You'll get the most favorable of terms no matter what you're asking for because your credit history and numbers have already told them that you're a mortal lock to repay it in full and on time.

HOW DO I BUILD GOOD PERSONAL CREDIT?

Building, or in many cases, rebuilding good credit is different for people at different stages of their life. We're going to start with the youngest group of people who are likely just starting off and work our way up the chain to people who have had some credit struggles and are attempting to fight their way back up to the surface, then build from there.

WHEN YOU'RE JUST STARTING OUT

If you're fresh out of high school, college, or just doing things on your own for the first time, now is a great time to get your credit score headed in the right direction. In this section we'll talk about ways to build credit with and without a credit card. Credit cards are quite obviously tied intricately to your credit score, but there are considerable risks in owning one. The average American between 18-24 already has about $2,000 worth of credit-card debt, and that number usually doubles within five years.

Open a credit card account: This gets you into the system and every day forward is the maturing of this first account. Make small purchases that you can easily repay, and pay the full balance by the end of each month. Even if you're just buying a tank of gas each month, pay it off and it will be reported positively.

Open a secured credit card account: This differs from a normal credit card in that is tied to your savings account, and the limit on the card is a direct reflection of the amount in the account. Just like a normal card, make small purchases and pay them off on time.

Open a joint credit card account or become an authorized user on someone else's account: This is the ideal-type situation for a college student leaving home or perhaps joining the military. You aren't the primary card holder, but you can still make purchases and payments on it, and it will be reported to the credit bureaus under your name. Make sure you make all your payments in a timely fashion, or it will hurt both yours and the real account holders' credit scores. Becoming an authorized account user is an increasingly popular tactic known as "piggybacking credit." If a person with good credit accepts you as an authorized user of their credit card, their payment history becomes your payment history. Even if you just turned 18 years old last week, if they've had the card for 15 years, your credit history will say you've had a positive payment history for 15 years as well. Of course if you abuse the authorized account or if the primary account holder falls behind on payments, your credit score will also be affected.

There are a couple of downsides to this kind of arrangement. For starters, not every credit card company reports your authorized status to the three major credit bureaus. Secondly, you're not going to learn anything about creating and maintaining good credit habits by just piggybacking off of someone else's lifetime of hard work. It's a bit like graduating high school and being hired the next day by the company one of your parents works for. You have no idea what you're doing, and if you don't learn quickly it's likely to blow up in your face sooner rather than later.

There are also for-profit piggybacking services that seek out consumers who are looking to build credit. These firms will sell you an authorized account with a total stranger who has a great credit score. You pay a fee for a select time period and benefit off their good history. This service has tremendous risks, however: It's a questionable business practice that is considered bank fraud in some instances; it is really expensive, as much as $4,000; you have to give away your personal information to a less than reputable company; and it's only a short-term solution. It can also cast you in a bad light with future creditors. If you're 25 years old and seeking a loan for a car, and your credit report shows you have had a Mastercard with excellent payment history for the past 20 years, banks officials tend to get suspicious.

Keep up with your student loans: Student loans seem terrific when you first get them and suddenly you have enough money to chase your academic dreams. They're not so much fun when you graduate and face five-digit loan balances. You don't have to pay them off in record time, you just have to pay them off. Make your payment on time each month to build your credit.

Take out a car loan: You might have saved enough money to buy a new or used car already, but if not you can take out an auto installment loan. Make sure it's a vehicle you can afford, not just something that you want. If you have saved money for a down payment, you have alot more negotiating power in terms of the length of the lease and how much interest rates and monthly payments are. Seeing the loan through to completion and paying on time each month are great ways to give your personal credit a strong base.

Obtain a secured loan: Sometimes you need money for things besides cars when you're first starting out, say the down payment on an apartment or tools for your profession if you're an artist, a gardener, or an architect. Secure loans are low-risk loans that give you the funds you need now and help you build credit as you pay them back.

Get credit for what you pay: There are services that will post your apartment rental payments to your credit report. Some credit bureaus will do the same for bills like cell phone charges and utilities to show you are paying what you owe every month. Explore your options to get rewarded for living up to your financial commitments.

WHEN YOU'RE OFF TO A GOOD START

If you've started off your life away from home with good choices and good credit, congratulations! You're ahead of the curve. But when you want to augment your credit score, particularly if you're angling to apply for a small business loan, there are several tips you can follow to get the ball rolling.

Request a credit-limit increase: Let's say your first credit card had a limit of $1,000. Every month you charge about $100 worth of purchases on it and pay it all off. Then your car breaks down and you have to put a repair charge of $750 on your credit card. You can't pay it all off in one month and the balance sits for a while, causing your debt-to-credit limit ratio to skyrocket to 75%. If you've been consistently paying off your balance month to month, there's no reason why your provider should not raise your limit, as you've proven you are a consistent re-payer. Call and explain the situation. If they raise your limit to $5,000, your debt-to-credit limit percentage drops back down to a very solid 15%.

Space out your credit-card applications: If you're applying for credit cards every month or two, it makes you look bad, like you're trying to use one to pay off another, or you're just in a shopping frenzy. Space out applications to at least once every six months, and don't apply for one if you know you're coming up on applying for a home loan or a car note.

WHEN YOU'RE STRUGGLING

Let's be honest, most people don't think that much about their credit score until they realize it's restricting them from getting something they want, like a small business, car, or house loan. By that time, you might have a bunch of missed payments on a credit card where you got in over your head. You might have missed a payment on your mortgage or your car and now you're struggling to get back to level ground. Whatever the reason is, your biggest objective now is keeping your credit score from dropping any lower. To make that happen you need to ensure three things:

- Don't miss any payments
- Don't close any accounts
- Don't open any more credit-card accounts until your score starts going up.

Every time you miss a payment, your credit score takes a hit. You have to arrange your finances so that stops. If you've suffered some sort of a hardship like a medical emergency or a natural disaster, call your credit-card company and let them know, they may have waivers or other triggers in place that can help you get back on your feet again.

Only close an account if there's no way you'll ever be able to pay it off. Why? Because doing so can hurt your credit score. Unless it's a very new account, closing a credit-card account can lower the average age of your accounts, which makes you a weaker candidate for sustainability.

Finally, if you're trying to keep opening more accounts, it gives the impression that you're just piling up more debt - either you're trying to transfer balances or you're using a new credit card to pay off your latest bills.

02:

BUSINESS/CORPORATE CREDIT

If you want to open your own business, regardless of what industry it's in or how big (or small) you want to be, you're very likely going to need help, most likely in the form of a loan, but perhaps more than one or as a background check of sorts from a variety of different potential partners. That's where business credit, also known as corporate credit, comes into play. This chapter will explore what business credit is, what you can use it for, and how to build and maintain it.

WHAT IS IT?

Just like what we discussed in Chapter 1 on personal credit, business credit is the track record of your business's financial dealings, particularly how reliable you are when it comes to lending you money or doing business with you. There is nothing secretive about your business credit, it all derives from public records including:

- Outstanding balances
- Payment habits
- Size of your business
- Age of your business
- Liens
- Bankruptcies

Just like your personal credit, there is a score affixed to your business credit. There are numerous agencies that calculate this score and each has a different method, but most stay on a scale ranging from 0-100. Just like in school, if your score is 80 or higher you are considered to have "good" credit and will be more successful.

Here's a quick explanation of how three agencies calculate your business credit score:

Equifax uses three factors to give clients an idea of your business's risk level. The first is a credit risk, which weighs the chance that your business becomes extremely delinquent; the second is a business failure score, which calculates the likelihood that your business will close; and the third is a payment index, which determines how likely you are to make all your payments on time.

Dun & Bradstreet has cultivated a system called PAYDEX, which gives a score from 1-100 based on all the information on your business that Dun & Bradstreet has on its servers.

Experian, which like Equifax is also a leading consumer credit score provider, also gives a score from 1-100 from several criteria, including: payment history, new lines of credit opened, and years you've been in business.

There's a fourth credit score that small business owners should know about, particularly if they are looking to employee the services of the Small Business Administration (SBA). FICO - our old friend from the consumer credit score reports - also maintains the Small Business Scoring Service (SBSS). The job of the SBSS is to rank your business on its ability to make on-time payments. This is important because the SBA has the power to make offer term loans, commercial loans, and lines of credit up to $350,000. You need a minimum score of 140 on a scale running from 0-300 to pre-qualify for the good stuff.

WHAT DO I NEED IT FOR?

You may be the type of entrepreneur who believes he or she will never need to worry about business credit because you have no plans on ever needing more money than you already have to run your business. For instance, if you are a freelance graphic artist, you can work from your home office and don't really need anything more than a computer with the standard graphic artist software tools (such as Adobe Illustrator and Adobe Photoshop) on it. Since just about everyone works digitally these days, you don't really have to worry about printing anything out, so your costs are basically just the electricity bill that powers your devices. But if you're good at what you do, your business is going to grow. That might mean investing in software and hardware upgrades for your home office. It might mean hiring a couple other graphic artists to take on your lower-level jobs while you focus on the big-job clients. If you're really successful locally, it might mean opening a brick-and-mortar location where clients can come in and discuss work with you in person rather than via email, it might even mean advertising online, partnering with other businesses, or investing in cloud server space to launch a powerful business website and accompanying portfolio. These things all take money. And just because you're doing well does not mean you should pay everything upfront when you want to expand. Business loans, lines of credit, and other financial instruments can allow you to make big purchases and pay them off gradually. Not only is this less risky, but it also builds up more business credit and presents you as a sound business partner.

WHAT YOU DON'T KNOW ABOUT BUSINESS CREDIT CAN HURT YOU

As this book and the rest of this series will show you, it's quite astonishing how much the average person does not know about starting and running a small business. Don't believe us? A recent survey shows that 45% of business owners aren't even aware they have a business credit score, and 72% don't know what it means. That's a serious problem for those seeking to secure any kind of financing. You need to know everything about your business if you're going to make it work, and that especially rings true when it comes to the financial end of things. Nearly one-half of people who get turned down for some sort of business loan don't know why. And a lack of financing or running out of money is the reason that three-fourths of businesses fail. Having good business credit makes just as much sense as having good personal credit. Even if you don't expect to use it any time soon, you never know when circumstances will change and you'll want or need it.

ESTABLISHING BUSINESS CREDIT

Depending on what kind of business you're running, you might be tempted to just use your personal credit score for your business. But separating the two has lots of advantages. By having a business credit history apart from your personal one, you guarantee that negative events in one world or the other don't affect both. If you're in the beginning steps of a business and you miss a couple of car note payments, you don't want your personal problems to have a bad effect on your ability to get a business loan down the line.

Separating your business and credit scores means officially incorporating your business. We'll discuss that in detail in Chapter 4, but we advised there are fees and licenses and wait times involved. However, it also does a great deal to protect you and your family's personal assets from any legal ramifications or potential lawsuits that could be brought against your business. Establishing your business credit can be done in eight steps. It won't be a quick process, but if you take it step by step, you can build that strong base and start doing business with the confidence that if you need to take out a loan or establish a line of credit, you've got the foundation to do it with.

STEP #1: INCORPORATE YOUR BUSINESS

As mentioned briefly above, officially declaring what you're doing as a business such as an LLC legall separates you from your business and tells the government and the various reporting agencies that this new entity is in need of a business credit score.

STEP #2: OBTAIN A FEDERAL TAX IDENTIFICATION NUMBER

More commonly known as an EIN, this number works about the same as your own social security number, in that it tracks pretty much everything your business is legally doing. You'll use your EIN when you file taxes on your business or when you open a business bank account with the name of your business instead of your name on it. If your business gets big, you might also need to use it to pay vendors for services provided - we'll cover that in a later volume.

STEP #3: OPEN YOUR FIRST BUSINESS BANK ACCOUNT

This means the bank account has your company's

name on it, not your name. Whenever you pay for something that is specifically going to be for your business, it will come out of this account.

STEP #4: ESTABLISH A BUSINESS PHONE NUMBER

This might seem a little prehistoric in the age of smartphones, texts, FaceTime, and the like, but it is another step in establishing your business as a separate entity from your personal life. Do you really want your mother-in-law calling on the same phone number you're trying to lock down long-term clients on? Even if your business and personal lives blend a lot, even a Voice over Internet Protocol (VoIP) or landline at your home that you never answer but dial business calls on is sufficient.

STEP #5: OPEN A BUSINESS CREDIT FILE

This isn't like your personal credit history where it just happens naturally. You need to open the file with the big three credit agencies: Experian, Equifax, and TransUnion. That gets them checking out your business and assigning you a score. Banks, business partners, and others can look up your business score to determine how solid you are with taking care of the financial end of your business.

STEP #6: OPEN A BUSINESS CREDIT CARD ACCOUNT

You don't have to go overboard with credit cards, in fact you don't have to use the one you open more than a single purchase a month if you don't need to. However, having a credit card that reports to one of the big three credit agencies - which is pretty much every credit card you've ever heard of - starts a trail for them to follow you. It also further differentiates your business from you the person. Just like with a personal credit card, if you don't need it, just make a couple of small purchases a month on your business card and pay them on time. It might seem silly on the surface to pull out a different credit card when you're buying a ream of paper or pack of 100 pencils, but by doing that and then paying it off in a timely fashion, you're tickling the fancy of the algorithms that help determine your business credit score, letting them know that "Business X" has a credit card, uses it monthly, and always pays its bill on time.

STEP #7: ESTABLISH A LINE OF CREDIT WITH VENDORS OR SUPPLIERS

This step really deviates from the rest of the advice on this page. The digital environment that so much commerce travels through is not the same as the one many of us grew up in: thousands of businesses have no physical product you can put your hands on. If you're a freelance copywriter, you're not going to have vendors or suppliers for a business because your business is writing words. So clearly this step is not for you. But if you're providing physical realm services or products, this is the part where you really separate your business from yourself. Say you make custom wedding cakes for your business. Your home kitchen might be your work kitchen, but your supplies - special types of icing, frosting, and cake batter along with all the decorations, aren't the type of things you can buy at the corner market. Buying small amounts from specialty stores is going to be too pricey, which is where you negotiate with the supplier on a line of credit where you can buy larger amounts at better prices and pay off your account on a regular basis.

STEP #8: PAY YOUR BILLS EVERY MONTH

Even if it means your personal take-home is way less, never, ever fail to pay a bill that your business owes on time. The minute you stiff a vendor, even by a single day, or don't hit this month's loan payment, your business credit score will suffer, and perhaps even worse, so will your reputation. It truly is one of the most difficult parts of running your own business: Realizing that everyone expects you to do exactly what you say exactly when you say it, and when you don't, they get very frustrated, very quickly.

MAINTAINING GOOD BUSINESS CREDIT

The above steps are huge parts of getting your business established and seen in a good light for potential creditors. But the journey does not stop there. Here are some great tips and tricks to maintain a good business credit score or even build it hire and hire over time.

Pay Early: That's right, as great as it is to pay your bills on time, paying them before they are due is even better. Some credit reports give something akin to extra credit for paying faster than is necessary. Do this whenever possible and watch your score rise.

Keep Your Information Current with the Credit Bureaus: If you move, if you change phone numbers, if you change company names, you need to let the big credit bureaus know about it. Why? Because they are not perfect, they are in charge of tens of thousands of business credit scores every day, and because they make mistakes, even as more and more of their processes become automated. Therefore if your company - Ray's Graphic Design - is located in Dallas, Texas at your house, but you end up setting up an actual brick-and-mortar location in nearby Arlington, TX, there's a real chance that the credit bureaus won't make the connection and think a new business has emerged in Arlington. Left unchecked, it can easily split your credit score in two - leaving your original "real" business with one score and starting a second file - and a second score - for what it believes to be a new business. That will kill your momentum and report your score inaccurately to lenders.

Check your Score at the Major Bureaus every few months: Like we said earlier, the bureaus make mistakes just like the rest of us, and the only way to keep them honest is to double-check your work. Say you pay your business loan annual payment on the Friday before a holiday weekend, but some downtime on the bank server doesn't register it until the following Tuesday. Your payment might be listed as late and your business credit score takes a hit accordingly, even though you paid on time. When something like this happens, you need to see it as soon as possible, no three years later when you're applying for a loan and can't figure out what happened.

Borrow Responsibly: One of the worst problems growing companies have is the idea that they need EVERYTHING NOW. Taking out loans or applying for a business credit card should be done only when you something is absolutely essential to your business moving forward, there's no work-around for it, and you don't have enough capital on hand to buy it yourself. In our freelance graphic artist example from above, if you started your business a month ago and you've already received 13 orders, when your computer suffers a hard drive crash, buying a new one with the best software becomes a must-have. It might cost $3,000 to get the right computer with the software features you need and the available processing power and RAM to keep you moving swiftly from job to job. For some businesses, $3,000 is no big deal, but for a startup it can look as big as Pikes Peak. Thus, a small business loan from a bank or the opening of a credit-card account to pay for the expense becomes absolutely necessary. If you're the same graphic artist five years down the road and you've just opened a small physical office for meeting with customers, you might get a happy trigger finger on that same credit card and be tempted to buy a fancy coffee machine, ergonomic chairs, and a flat screen TV for the comfort of you and your staff. But from the outside looking in, we can clearly see those are not needs, just creature comforts that don't actually contribute to the overall success of the business. Learn to know the difference or run the risk of overspending and (pun intended) paying for it.

03:

DEBT REDUCTION

It's not surprising that 'Debt' is a four-letter word. It is often the cause of lots and lots of swearing, frustration, and sleepless nights. Debt happens to people old and young, black and white, to those with Masters degrees and those with high school diplomas, those who make $20,000 per year and those that make $200,000 a year. It doesn't matter who you are, where you're from, or what you do for a living. Debt is a part of life for just about everyone. If you are smart with your money and your decision-making processes, not to mention more than a little lucky, debt will be a manageable part of your life that will help you earn a good credit score, acquire the things you need in life, and be able to stay financially upright. If you are not smart with your money, don't follow the old adage of "saving for a rainy day", and do not make good decisions, your debt runs the risk of becoming unmanageable and become a huge weight on your ability to do what you want, financially or otherwise, and cost you enormously over the long term. Not being able to manage your debt can lead you into a debt cycle, which will be discussed below, do major damage to your personal and/or business credit scores, and see you potentially lose assets like your car or home. The solution to this is debt reduction, a strict, steady way to get yourself out from underneath the yoke of being in debt.

WHAT CAUSES PEOPLE TO GO INTO DEBT?

Loosely defined, debt means any money you owe to another entity that you haven't paid yet. So theoretically, if the kid next door has a lemonade stand and only accepts exact change, you're in debt to him until you can break a $20 to give him two quarters for a cup of the good stuff. There are lots of kinds of debt in the world, and even good debt, as we've discussed in the previous chapters on building your personal and business credit scores. Very few people do not experience debt in their lifetimes. If you never do, you're either independently wealthy or own your own land and grow your own food. For the other 99.99% of us, debt is a reality. The rest of the world earns an income that affords them the ability to live a certain lifestyle.

When they want something beyond that, they have to either save up for it, or go into debt to purchase it, and then pay the debt off over time - almost always with interest.

There are pros and cons to this, of course. If you're wanting to buy a house for your family of four, it's fairly unreasonable to save up money for 15-20 years to pay cash for it. The more sensible thing to do is save for a few years to be able to build up a nice down payment, then apply for a home loan. The cost of the house minus your down payment becomes your debt. But assuming you know how much house you can afford and never miss a mortgage payment, this is a good debt, because it tells other lenders that you have the qualifications to secure a home loan and the means to pay it off like clockwork.

You have your home, the bank has its payments, everybody's happy.

Bad debt comes with poor financial decisions. If you graduate from college and get your first job making $50,000 per year, you might want to celebrate and buy a new car. Your credit score is probably OK, and given your salary, a car dealership will be more than happy to sell you the most flashy, cherry-red, fast-driving roadster on its lot, and assure you that you can make the monthly payments no problem.

That might even be the case, at least until the realities of living your life set in, and you have to factor in auto insurance, gas, all your new utility bills, your rent, the various deductions from your paycheck for taxes and insurance, any vacations you want to take, and all those unexpected expenses that pop up that you don't remember having to worry about as a kid.

That's when our $750/month car payment starts to look like an anchor dragging you down instead of the visual representation of freedom.

Cars and houses are on most people's wish lists and the most common single purchases that lead to debt, but properly managed, they are also the smartest reasons to go into debt.

That leads us to the #1 reason that most people go into debt: Poor financial decisions centered around credit cards.

THE STARK REALITIES OF CREDIT CARD DEBT

Credit-card debt is such a killer in the US that government leaders and educators alike have discussed making education on the subject part of public school curriculum. Credit cards are great for what they are intended for - helping you purchase items you need now that are more than you can afford at one time. They are terrible when they are misused, feeding into the individual mindset of "I want what I want, and I want it now." While the overwhelming share of the blame is on the individual, credit card companies are hardly guiltless in the grand scheme of things. Their television commercials show people on tropical beaches and enjoying once-in-a-life experiences thanks to their credit cards. They're given names like "Freedom" with the idea that a credit card can make all your dreams come true, and they are layered with "rewards programs" that insist that buying more and more is the way to go, because you'll get cash back or all sorts of fun prizes, free airplane trips, and hotel stays.

If you're spending within your means, all of that is actually true. Using a credit card when you need it and paying it off will ultimately award you some nice loyalty bonuses. But when viewed as a race to see who gets the most points first, it is a very slippery slope.

But like we said, we can't blame the credit card companies - after all, they're trying to accomplish the same thing as everyone else, make money and be successful businesses. We, the individual consumers, are the ones making the bad decisions. Using credit cards to fund vacations we can't afford, to "keep up with the Joneses" by purchasing more things for our home we know are out of our budget, And it's not just the buying that does people in, it's the lack of understanding on how credit cards work. How many people have been lured into the promise of a credit card with zero interest for the first 12 months, but never read the fine print about after that first year, the interest rate is 17%? It's situations like this when people get trapped in a debt cycle and can never work their way out, because they've accrued so much debt that only paying each month's minimum payment is never going to be enough.

According to financial website NerdWallet, the average American household has credit card debt of $15,482. When you weigh that against US median household income of $59,039, and realize that most people also have at least one car note and possibly a mortgage payment as well, you can obviously see how serious the credit-card debt issue is.

BREAKING DOWN THE DEBT CYCLE

The debt cycle is simple to understand from the outside, but devastating to experience from the inside. Countless people enter it believing it will be a one-time thing, only to find themselves repeating it month after month until it becomes the only reality they know.

Breaking the cycle, which is discussed at length in the sections to follow, is a process that takes rigorous honesty, objective planning, and righteous self-control. It usually also takes a considerable amount of time, which is one of many reasons so many people struggle to maintain it. That's for a bit later, first we will go over the cycle before we begin to discuss how to break free of it.

STEP 1: NOT ENOUGH MONEY FOR THE PURCHASES YOU NEED/WANT TO MAKE

Everyone is familiar enough with this step. You've reached a point in the month where your next paycheck is far away and your financial needs or wants have a much shorter shelf life. Whether it's paying the electricity bill, paying off a credit card for the month, or something more impulsive like buying new shoes or a new smartphone, our brains have made the decision that this is the next necessary financial step, whether that's true or not.

STEP 2: MAKING THOSE PURCHASES VIA CREDIT CARD

When the bank account says no, the credit card is almost always to step in and cry out "Yes, please!" It's quite amazing how we always seem to know exactly how much wiggle room we have on every credit card, even when we've sworn off ever using them again until the balance is under control. With the rise of ecommerce and the kind of shipping that guarantees next-day delivery, impulse buying is even more out of control than it ever was when department stores stacked their most popular items by the register where they were so easy to grab and buy. Temptation is everywhere for the weak-willed consumer. You can do irrevocable damage to your bank account and credit score without moving out of your favorite spot on the couch with a smartphone and a few choice websites.

STEP 3: CREDIT-CARD BALANCES GROW

If you're not paying off your credit card bill every month, a credit-card purchase is never a one-time thing. There's the initial purchase of course, but if you have not paid it off at the end of the next billing cycle, it becomes part of your balance which is charged whatever your current interest rate is. Let's say your "can't wait, must have" item for this week is a new purse that you saw someone at work sporting last week. It's $250, and you've already spent your personal items budget for the month, but you've decided another weekend simply cannot go by without this purse on your arm, so you figure out which of your credit cards has $250 of available credit and punch the numbers into Amazon's website. You've got your new bag in less than 24 hours and the world is right again. So now you owe an additional $250 to your credit card, but since you're already over your budget for the month, it's not going to get paid off come the first of the month. When that happens, your credit card will exercise the 17% interest rate on your existing balance. A 17% charge on a $250 purse is $42.50, meaning now that new purse has cost you $292.50. If you don't pay it off next month, the 17% will hit again and the purse will now cost $342.23. On and on and on it goes.

STEP 4: BIGGER BALANCES, HIGHER MINIMUM PAYMENTS

As your credit card balances go up and the interest with them, your minimum payments for those credit cards will rise as well. In fact lots of people quickly run into the scenario where the interest charged on their account every month is more than the minimum balance due. So every time they make the minimum payment, it's not affecting the overall balance of their account at all, it's just covering some or all of the interest rates. You don't have to be a rocket scientist to realize that if you never pay down the principal of a loan, you'll be in debt forever.

STEP 5: HIGHER PAYMENTS, SAME INCOME

When your credit card bills go up, your paycheck covers fewer and fewer of your expenses. That makes for a very large dilemma: Pay your credit card bills or pay your "real-world" bills like the rent, groceries, car note, utilities, etc. Both choices have consequences, but the overarching one leads you right back to Step 1: Not having enough money for the purchases you want/need. The cycle has begun again.

HOW TO REDUCE YOUR DEBT

Reducing your debt is neither fun nor easy. But by understanding why you're in debt, cultivating a plan to reduce your debt, and following through on it, you will lower and eventually eradicate the amount of debt you owe. That is the equivalent of a second chance at making your dreams come true and should be cause for celebration. Before we begin the process of reducing debt, we must begin at the beginning and understand how you got into debt in the first place.

UNDERSTAND YOUR DEBT HISTORY

This is where the rigorous honesty and transparency begins. Getting trapped in a debt cycle doesn't happen overnight and ringing up so much credit-card debt that you can no longer pay your bills doesn't happen by accident. Both are the result of a series of bad financial decisions, almost always as a result of buying things you cannot afford, either via credit-card use or taking out a car loan or house loan that you ultimately cannot afford to pay along with the rest of your bills. Some people would rather not delve too far into the reasons why they are in debt, but it's an essential step to take in order to not repeat it during the debt reduction process, and especially when you are debt free again.

This means reviewing your bank statements and credit-card statements, along with your paycheck stubs to see at one point you started getting in over your head on keeping up with your bills. It might have been something legitimate, like losing a job or getting sick and having to pay exorbitant medical bills. But how you responded to those challenges is what determines why your debt might have gotten out of hand. Losing a job does not mean continuing on in your normal spending habits as if income was still coming in twice a week.

Being able to be flexible and understand the cause and effect of various situations is paramount in understanding your current debt situation.

More often than not, debt gets out of control when we make bigger purchases than we can afford or continuously buy the things we want on credit cards while paying our other bills with money from our bank account. When it comes time to paying our suddenly higher credit-card minimum balances, there's no money in the bank account and we end up being decked with late fees and interest charges we can't afford.

As you begin to discover the history of your debt, use a notebook or a combination of word processor and spreadsheet to pinpoint the events and results of the things that created your debt situation. Look for patterns of behavior. Was your paycheck inconsistent and you kept having to dip into your emergency fund or credit cards to pay for basic items? Do you find yourself ringing up credit card expenses to do things outside of your budget, like meals out with coworkers or buying new outfits for work? This isn't about judging your motivations and your decisions, this is a fact-finding mission to move forward in the debt-reduction process.

WANTS VS. NEEDS

Now it's time to start the heavy lifting. You'll need some time for this one, so don't try to cram it in during your lunch break or while waiting in the car pickup line at your kids' school. Pen, paper, and your last 30 days of bank statements, either printed out or on a computer screen.

Every single transaction on your bank statement needs to be filed as either as Need (N) or a Want (W). It's just as simple as that - things you need to buy go in one column, and things you want to buy go in the other. This is where things can tricky and you'll need to take a deep look at your priorities.

The only things that should be in your "Need" category are true essentials such as your rent/mortgage, your car note, your utilities, any debt payments you have, your grocery bill, gas for your car, food for your pets, medical appointments, prescription medicine, and things like monthly allowances for new clothes for your kids.

Everything else goes into the "Want" category. This includes things you might have come to think of as needs such as a cable TV package with all the movie channels; a morning trip to Starbucks for a pre-work mocha frappuccino; or $100/month for eating lunch out with your friends.

Those things are not Needs; they are Wants. Every single one of them could go away and you would still be able to live and work without difficulties. You might not like it nearly as much, but you can certainly do it.

Once you've got your two categories separated, add them up and write down the totals. Now add up all the money that comes into your bank account in a month: whatever you and/or your spouse make plus any other passive forms of income like dividend checks, money from renting property, profit from a side gig, etc.

LIVING BELOW YOUR MEANS

The things in your "Wants" column are going to be going away for a while, but not forever. And probably don't have to sacrifice all of them all the time, but you do need to be prepared for some very drastic cuts.

The next step is to compare the total of your monthly "Needs" column to that of your monthly "Income" column. If Your income is the greater total, pat yourself on the back. You have the opportunity to live below your means, which basically translates into paying all your essential bills every month without needing to put anything on a credit card.

The rest of your money, including most or all of what you have been spending on "Wants" needs to head for two new destinations: 1) An emergency funds account and 2) Bigger payments to get rid of your accrued debt.

Now let's be honest. Living below your means is a very different experience then ringing up whatever you happen to want at the time on credit cards and worrying about the consequences later. Unfortunately, "later" always comes, and can cost you years of financial and mental anguish if you don't get in front of the problem before it gets really out of control. Long-term consequences can include having to declare for bankruptcy; losing your house or your car; seeing your credit score drop so low that it will be virtually impossible to ever qualify for a loan again; and having to rely on family to support you and your own family.

REDUCING YOUR DEBT

Now that you've got a plan in place to eliminate unnecessary expenses and use that extra money to save for a rainy day / pay off debt, it's time to look at the damages. Gather statements for every account you owe money on and line them all up. Use your journal and write down how much is due on every account, what the payment date is, what the interest rate is, and how much the minimum balance is.

There are two ways to go forward from here. One is the snowball method made very popular by American financial advisor and author Dave Ramsey. The other makes more sense mathematically, but definitely does not have the same power of momentum that Ramsey's method does. Both ways have their positives and negatives as will be discussed below. In the long run, the right method is the one that works best for you and your family to maintain a positive attitude and efficiently work towards reducing your debt. For both methods, we're going to use the same example so you can see each one works.

DEBT REDUCTION EXAMPLE

To demonstrate the two examples, we've created a 35-year-old single female named Callye. Callye works as a marketing executive and rents an apartment. She's got a car note, but too much credit-card spending early in her life has seen her debt overwhelm her in the past few years to where she's never paying more than the minimum balance, and that's barely covering the interest charges on her account.

When Callye breaks down her Needs, Wants, and Income, she finds that her Needs total $4,500 per month: That includes the minimum payments to her credit-card accounts. By eliminating 90% of the things on her Wants list, she's able to free up an extra $200/month. Callye has four credit cards with balances on them. They are:

- A Home Depot card with $400 on it, a $50 minimum payment and an interest rate of 5%.
- A Visa card with $2,000 on it, a $150 minimum payment, and an interest rate of 10%.
- A Best Buy card with $800 on it, an $80 minimum payment, and an interest rate of 8%.

- A MasterCard with $5,000 on it, a $500 minimum payment, and an interest rate of 15%.

THE SNOWBALL METHOD

In the Snowball Method championed by Ramsey and praised by tens of thousands of former debt sufferers, Callye should start with the card with the lowest amount on it and pay it off first. So in Month 1, she pays all of her normal monthly balances off, and pays an extra $200 to the Home Depot card. That knocks its balance down from $400 to $150 (plus interest).

By the time the second month is complete, she has paid the Home Depot card off completely. Her next target is the Best Buy card ($800). She's knocked down that total some with two monthly payments of $80, but seen it move back up some too thanks to the 8% interest rate. With Home Depot in the books, she now takes the $80 minimum payment for Best Buy plus her $200/month extra savings, plus $50/month from her Home Depot minimum payment that is no longer required. $200+$50+80 = $330. Callye now has $330/month to use on her Best Buy car. She's able to pay it off within 2-3 months.

Her next stop is her Visa card with $2,000 on it. It's been a push-pull on this account while she's paying off the first two, but she's moved the balance down some. And the good news is that her $150 minimum payment now has an additional $330 added to it, bumping it up to $480/month. By keeping locked into her habits, within a year of starting her debt reduction program, she's taken all of her principal off the Visa card and put three of her four cards down to zero balances.

That just leaves the MasterCard ($10,000). She's diligently made her $500/month payments over the past 12 months. Unfortunately with that enormous annual percentage rate (APR), she's taking on water fast. The APR is how much a credit-card company charges you per year when you have an unpaid balance from month to month. To figure it out on a monthly basis, you take the APR - 15% and divide it by the number of days in a year 365 to get 0.41%. Now less than half of one percent might not seem like a lot if your balance is $200, but Callye's is $10,000. That means she's being charged $20.50 PER DAY for her balance of $10,000. That's more than $600 per month in interest alone. Suddenly her $500 minimum balance payment don't seem so impressive. If roughly 12 months have gone by since she started the Snowball Method, her MasterCard balance has snowballed in the wrong direction. In the first month, her balance goes up $135 based on $635 of interest versus as $500 minimum payment. By the end of the year, Callye's balances has climbed well above where it was a year ago. At this point, she can start devoting $980/month to it. This will allow her to go above the interest charges and begin knocking down the actual balance a few hundred dollars per month. It will take many years, but eventually she will reach her goal.

Ramsey's system is great for morale because you are seeing results almost immediately by knocking out small debts first and then rapidly speeding up your payment of medium-sized ones thanks to bigger payments. But the downside is apparent if you have high-balance, high-APR cards that get stuck at the end of the strategy. When that occurs, you run the risk of adding a lot of years and a whole lot of extra dollars to your debt reduction plan, although paying it off in big chunks after all the other accounts have been settled will feel like a victory.

THE HIGHEST INTEREST RATE METHOD

In the Snowball Method championed by Ramsey and praised by tens of thousands of former debt sufferers definitely has its merits, but mathematics shows it is inferior to this method in terms of time taken and dollars spent.

The Highest Interest Rate method is based on the idea that whichever card has the highest interest rate must be paid off first, because it is the one costing you the most money on a month-to-month basis.

In this method, Callye would pay off her accounts in reverse order from the Snowball Method. While she would not see quick results right away, she'll be saving herself time and money on the back end of the deal.

Using this method, Callye immediately adds the $200 extra/month to the $500 she is spending on her Mastercard bill. Her initial payments will not knock down the $10,000 payment down in big chunks like the other method will, but it will keep the initial balance from skyrocketing every month based on that huge APR. By comparison, her smaller interest-rate cards will not go up nearly as quickly in principal. The Home Depot card ($400) might only take two months to pay off in the Snowball Method, but it's such a small amount it does not matter much in the grand scheme of things. At a 5% APR, those $400 are only increasing by just 54 cents per day. Compare that to the $20.50 that the big Mastercard was rising by each day at its 15% APR in the Snowball Method. This minute charges on the lower interest rates means a lot less money to pay off in the long run by tackling the most challenging obstacle first. Once it's paid off, Callye will be paying $700 per month to the next highest-interest rate. By the time she gets to the Best Buy and Home Depot cards, it might take 1-2 months to reduce them to zero balances.

04:

INCORPORATING YOUR BUSINESS

When you get serious about starting your own business or when your side hustle of part-time gig has become so big that you make it your full-time passion, it's time to go officially go into business. Doing that isn't just about printing up some cards and making a Facebook group for your customers. You need to decide on what kind of business structure fits the best for you.

There will be legal and financial ramifications no matter what you choose, so review the following choices and even consider contacting the SBA or a lawyer if you have more specific questions you need answered.

SOLE PROPRIETORSHIP

Want to make your business a sole proprietorship? Congratulations, it already is! Confused? Don't be. If you're doing any sort of business but not registered as a business, you're automatically qualified as a sole proprietorship. This means you don't have to pay for any sort of fees but it also means that you are personally responsible for any debts the business incurs. And if someone should happen to sue your business, your personal assets, such as money and property, are at risk.

PARTNERSHIPS

There are two common kinds of partnerships if you are being joined in your business with another person. The first is a limited partnership (LP) and the other one is a limited liability partnership (LLP).

An LP indicates that one partner has unlimited liability while all the others have limited liability.

This also means they have limited control over the company, something usually well-documented in a written agreement. Company profits are transferred to personal tax returns and the general partner must pay self-employment taxes as well.

An LLP means every owner has limited liability, meaning they aren't responsible for the actions of the other partners. If one of your partners takes all your investor seed money and bets it on the Cleveland

Browns to win the Super Bowl, the other partners are not liable to the investors when they want their money back.

LIMITED LIABILITY COMPANY (LLC)

An LLC is often considered to be the best of both worlds for small businesses as you get some of the best strengths of both a partnership arrangement and a corporate one. LLCs separate you from your business. If you face a lawsuit or a bankruptcy, no one can touch your personal possessions such as what's in your savings account or your kids' college fund, or your house. You also don't have to pay corporate taxes on profits or losses - those go straight to your personal income. It's not all wine and roses, however; if you are part of an LLC, you are considered to be self-employed and you must pay self-employment tax contributions towards Social Security and Medicare just like everyone else.

LIMITED LIABILITY PARTNERSHIP (LLP)

An LLP has a lot of the same characteristics as an LLC in that its has some qualities of corporations but each partner is not responsible for another partner's negligence.Unliked in a corporations, the partners can choose to manage the business themselves. LLPs also have a different level of tax liability. It is best suited for businesses in which investors want to be active in management, not passive and just funneling money with the hope for a healthy return on investment.

CORPORATIONS

You don't have to have a stodgy board of directors and 63 retail outlets in the tri-state area to become a corporation. A corporation is defined as any legal entity that is separate from its owners. A corporation has legal rights much like individuals, such as loaning and borrowing money, hiring employees, owning assets, creating contracts, suing, but also being sued.

There are a few different types of corporations that might apply to your business.

C CORP

A C Corp is the embodiment of the basic definition above. It offers the best protection to you, the owner, from personal liability, but there is a high cost to form one. You also will need to maintain reporting, record-keeping, and operational processes. Corporations pay income tax on their profits, but have the advantage of being able to raise capital for necessary investments through the sale of stock, which can also be used to attract employees. If you believe your business idea is the type that one day might need to "go public" to drive fund-raising, a C Corp is something you should greatly consider.

S CORP

S Corps are a lot like C Corps except that C Corps are often taxed twice for income, the second time being when dividends are passed onto shareholders. S Corps avoid this process by allowing both profits and some types of losses to go straight to the owners' personal income without being weighed down by corporate tax rates. Make sure the state you do business in recognizes S Corps, as it is not necessarily part of every state's laws.

B CORP

A benefit corporation, also known as a B Corp, are driven by both mission and profit, and they make public their purpose, accountability, and transparency, although they are taxed the same as a C Corp. Their shareholders make sure the company is producing not only a profit, but also something that benefits the public.

NON-PROFIT ORGANIZATIONS

Non-profits differ from all other types of business entities in that their primary purpose is to further a social cause or advocate united point of view. As such, any surplus of revenue does not go to investors' pockets or shareholders' stock value, but to take strides towards achieving its goals. Employees still draw salaries and the organizations are still considered incorporated. In the US, NPOs can file for tax-exempt status from federal income taxes by meeting certain requirements of the Internal Revenue Service.

ABOUT AUTHOR

Author, consultant, entertainment executive in both music and animation "Jzhamael Kebulon Ashantee" is a native angeleno entrepreneur that has spent the last twenty-five years in the business arena.

Always one to reach back in an attempt to serve the community in which he came from, he created urbanomics 101 as a method to take the lessons that he has learned, along with other prominent educators and business professionals directly to the innercity streets. The goal being to make the information available to those in areas that lack the resources needed to access mainstream america's pot of gold.

Coming from a religously diverse and agnostic family, the only thing that everyone could agree upon is that we need to rebuild businesses and wealth in the black communitities.

It was out of that spirit that urbanomics 101 was born!

-Jzhamael Kebulon Ashantee

www.ingramcontent.com/pod-product-compliance
Lightning Source LLC
Chambersburg PA
CBHW070830220526
45466CB00002B/789